Chaffinch

Look for this bright bird hopping across the frosty ground. It likes to peck up seeds from under hedges and bird tables.

Male (females are browner)

Small eyes and a pointed nose

Common shrew

You might spot it snuffling through dead leaves, hunting for insects and worms – it needs to eat every few hours to survive the winter.

Red, poisonous berries

Holly

Dark, spiky and loved by birds for the shelter it gives in winter. Its glossy leaves and bright berries are often used as festive decorations.

Towns and cities

Needles and berries are poisonous

Yew
You'll often find yew trees in quiet churchyards, watching over the graves. Some are over 1,000 years old.

Cat
Cats prowl through streets and gardens, on the lookout for an extra meal. Their thick fur helps protect them from the cold.

Black beak and legs

Pied wagtail
Often seen on pavements and in car parks. Its long tail bobs up and down as it skitters around looking for crumbs.

Feral pigeon

These birds gather in large flocks in parks and town squares. Listen for the low 'coo'ing calls as they fight over people's leftover lunch.

Shiny green and purple neck

London plane

Look for strings of spiky seed balls hanging down from its branches like little baubles. The bark has a patchy pattern.

Brown rat

Can live almost anywhere but thrives in busy cities. Its sensitive nose helps it sniff out seeds and scraps.

Parks

Short pointed needles

Norway spruce
You might spot one of these inside at Christmas, decked with sparkly lights and tinsel! But out in the wild they grow much taller.

Waxwing
Keep an eye out for its pink crest and yellow-tipped tail. It visits the UK in winter to feast on the last of the berries.

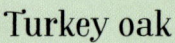

Turkey oak
Difficult to tell from other oaks in winter, but look closely and you'll see it has long 'whiskers' sprouting from its twigs.

Rough greyish bark

Sunburst lichen

This bright lichen grows on trees and stone walls. From a distance it looks like a splatter of yellow paint.

Common alder

Look for little brown cones dangling from its branches – birds snack on the small seeds inside. Often grows in damp soil.

Canada goose

You'll find flocks of these big geese around lakes and canals, honking loudly as they waddle beside the cold water.

Long black neck

Hedgerows

Hawthorn

A gnarled tree that grows low to the ground. Its hard red berries keep lots of little birds well fed during the winter months.

Stoat

If you're lucky, you might spot a stoat slinking through the hedgerows, hunting for mice and rabbits.

Fieldfare

Listen for its loud *chack-chack* call as it hops between bushes filled with berries. Often part of a noisy flock.

Speckled breast

Mistletoe

Look for bushy balls of mistletoe up in the branches of apple and hawthorn trees. At first glance, they look like a big bird's nest.

Poisonous leaves and berries

Reddish patch under wings

Redwing

Flits about the countryside in search of winter berries. If the snow gets too heavy, it might visit garden bird-feeders instead.

December moth

A fluffy little moth that flutters around on cold winter nights. Females lay their eggs on bark and twigs to hatch in the spring.

Heaths and moors

Kestrel
Hovers on the wind, scanning the fields below for mice and voles. Look for its long tail feathers that it fans out for balance.

Male (female has browner feathers)

Juniper
Grows on wild, windy moors. Its trunk is often twisted and bent, and its berries take two years to ripen.

Prickly leaves

Crowberry
A low-growing shrub with short, needle-like leaves. Look for clusters of dark berries dotted along its stems.

Ladybirds (hibernating)

As the days grow darker, ladybirds huddle together in sheltered spots to sleep through until spring. You might see a cluster of them tucked up under a leaf.

Grey winter coat

Sika deer

Lives in woods and on open heathland. Look for the male stag's antlers silhouetted against the sky.

Pixie cup lichen

These dainty cups sprout up on old logs and mossy rocks. They have a silvery tinge that makes them look frosty.

Farms and fields

Horse
Grows a thick winter coat to keep itself warm. Watch its breath steam as it bends its neck to the frosty grass.

Speckled breast

Mistle thrush
Nicknamed 'storm cock' because on windy days this big songbird likes to sing from the top of a swaying tree.

Dog rose
Red rosehips hang from the branches of this wild and rambling rose. They help feed birds and mice through the winter.

Thorns help it climb up other plants.

Sheep

They graze in large flocks, often on higher ground. Listen for their loud bleats calling back and forth over the fields.

Thick wool coat

Tiny eyes and a pink nose

Mole

The closest you'll probably get to spotting a mole is the little mounds of earth they leave behind as they tunnel for grubs and worms.

Bewick's swan

A small, elegant swan. Watch it gliding downriver, or picking its way across the nearby fields, looking for grain.

Rivers and wetlands

Lapwing
Large flocks gather on fields and wetlands in winter. Look for their rounded wingtips as they wheel overhead at dusk.

Males have a green eye-stripe.

Teal
A small duck with a clear, whistling call. Keep your eyes peeled for a flash of green on its wings as it flies low overhead.

Otter
Hunts for fish along rivers and coasts. Look for its broad face bobbing above the water before it dives out of sight.

Strong swimmer with webbed feet

Water vole

Tricky to spot, but look for a small burrow in the riverbank with a neat nibbled 'lawn' of grass by the entrance.

Blunt nose and furry tail

Winter heliotrope

Its pale pink flowers bloom along rivers and hedgerows in midwinter. Their sweet vanilla scent hangs in the cold air.

Grey heron

Stands hunched over the water, still as a statue. If you wait long enough, you might see it stab down to spear a fish with its beak.

Black head crest

Coasts

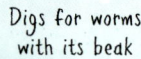
Digs for worms with its beak

Dunlin
They gather in huge flocks to feed along winter shores. Then as the tide comes in, they fly off to roost in fields and marshes.

Marram grass
Grows where the sand rises up into dunes. Its long grey-green tufts bend with the cold wind coming off the sea.

Dwarf gorse
Its small flame-like petals brighten the dark winter months. But watch out for its sharp green spines.

Great black-backed gull

A big, noisy bird that eats almost anything. Watch it strut about, grabbing food from other gulls or gulping down small animals whole.

Probes the sand with its long beak

Curlew

Easy to spot in winter – it's Europe's biggest wading bird. Listen for its eerie *cur-lee* call drifting over the water.

Deep root draws up fresh water

Sea kale

Grows high up on shingle beaches. Its leathery leaves used to be eaten by sailors to keep them healthy.

Woodlands

Snowdrops
These pale flowers bloom in the quiet winter woods. Their petals hang like icicles from delicate drooping stems.

Tawny owl
As dusk deepens, tawny owls emerge from their nests to hunt. Listen for the female's fierce *ki-wick* call, and the male's answering *hu-hooo*.

Often eaten by owls

Wood mouse
This tiny mouse mainly comes out at night. It hurries through the dark wood looking for berries and seeds to store in its burrow.

Blackthorn

A wiry, low-growing tree with thorny branches. Look for its dark juicy fruits in early winter. They're called 'sloes'.

The male's antlers look like horns.

Muntjac deer

This stocky little deer grazes on winter leaves and berries. It's nicknamed the 'barking deer' for its sharp, dog-like call.

Jelly ear fungus

Looks a bit like ears growing on a tree. Its jelly-like flesh is velvety on the outside and wrinkled on the inside.

Hills and mountains

Rowan

Often grows alone on a hill. Bunches of bright red berries hang from its branches and feed the moorland birds.

Ears have black tips

Mountain hare

Lives high in the hills and turns mostly white in winter to match the snow. But keep your eyes peeled for a pair of long, black-tipped ears.

Hairy leaves covered in sticky 'dew'

Round-leaved sundew

This tiny plant eats the little insects that live on boggy moors. Look for its hairy, sticky leaves wrapped around half-digested flies.

Highland cattle

Wild, ancient animals that live in the mountains all through winter. They use their horns to dig for fresh roots in the frozen earth.

Thick oily coat keeps it warm and dry

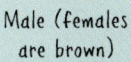

Male (females are brown)

Black grouse

Likes to live where the rolling moors meet open woodland. It grazes on leaves and winter berries, and shelters under the trees when the weather turns.

Reindeer moss

In the UK, this arctic plant is only found high in the mountains. It grows in thick, branching tufts from cracks in the icy rocks.

The pale branches look like reindeer antlers.

Spotting chart

Once you've spotted something from this book, find its sticker at the back, and stick it on this chart in the space below its name.

Bewick's swan	Black grouse	Blackthorn	Brown rat	Canada goose
Cat	Chaffinch	Common alder	Common beech	Common shrew
Crowberry	Curlew	December moth	Dog rose	Dunlin
Dwarf gorse	Feral pigeon	Fieldfare	Great black-backed gull	Grey heron
Hawthorn	Highland cattle	Holly	Horse	Jelly ear fungus

Juniper	Kestrel	Ladybirds	Lapwing	London plane
Marram grass	Mistle thrush	Mistletoe	Mole	Mountain hare
Muntjac deer	Norway spruce	Otter	Pied wagtail	Pixie cup lichen
Redwing	Reindeer moss	Robin	Round-leaved sundew	Rowan
Sea kale	Sheep	Sika deer	Snowdrops	Stoat
Sunburst lichen	Tawny owl	Teal	Turkey oak	Water vole
Waxwing	Winter heliotrope	Winter honeysuckle	Wood mouse	Yew

Index

Bewick's swan, 13
Black grouse, 21
Blackthorn, 19
Brown rat, 5

Canada goose, 7
Cat, 4
Chaffinch, 3
Common alder, 7
Common beech, 2
Common shrew, 3
Crowberry, 10
Curlew, 17

December moth, 9
Dog rose, 12
Dunlin, 16
Dwarf gorse, 16

Feral pigeon, 5
Fieldfare, 8

Great black-backed gull, 17
Grey heron, 15

Hawthorn, 8
Highland cattle, 21
Holly, 3

Horse, 12

Jelly ear fungus, 19
Juniper, 10

Kestrel, 10

Ladybirds, 11
Lapwing, 14
London plane, 5

Marram grass, 16
Mistle thrush, 12
Mistletoe, 9
Mole, 13
Mountain hare, 20
Muntjac deer, 19

Norway spruce, 6

Otter, 14

Pied wagtail, 4
Pixie cup lichen, 11

Redwing, 9
Reindeer moss, 21
Robin, 2

Round-leaved sundew, 20
Rowan, 20

Sea kale, 17
Sheep, 13
Sika deer, 11
Snowdrops, 18
Stoat, 8
Sunburst lichen, 7

Tawny owl, 18
Teal, 14
Turkey oak, 6

Water vole, 15
Waxwing, 6
Winter heliotrope, 15
Winter honeysuckle, 2
Wood mouse, 18

Yew, 4

First published in 2025 by Usborne Publishing Limited, 83–85 Saffron Hill, London EC1N 8RT, United Kingdom. usborne.com
Copyright © 2025 Usborne Publishing Limited. The name Usborne and the Balloon logo are trade marks of Usborne Publishing
Limited. All rights reserved. No part of this publication may be reproduced or used in any manner for the purpose of training artificial
intelligence technologies or systems (including for text or data mining), stored in retrieval systems or transmitted in any form or by
any means without prior permission of the publisher. Printed in China. UKE.